Carolin Kotthaus

The two faces of the character Blanche DuBois in "A Streetcar Named Desire"

GRIN Verlag

Bibliografische Information der Deutschen Nationalbibliothek:

Die Deutsche Bibliothek verzeichnet diese Publikation in der Deutschen National-
bibliografie; detaillierte bibliografische Daten sind im Internet über http://dnb.d-
nb.de/ abrufbar.

Imprint:

Copyright © 2010 GRIN Verlag GmbH
Druck und Bindung: Books on Demand GmbH, Norderstedt Germany
ISBN: 978-3-656-46161-6

GRIN - Your knowledge has value

Der GRIN Verlag publiziert seit 1998 wissenschaftliche Arbeiten von Studenten, Hochschullehrern und anderen Akademikern als eBook und gedrucktes Buch. Die Verlagswebsite www.grin.com ist die ideale Plattform zur Veröffentlichung von Hausarbeiten, Abschlussarbeiten, wissenschaftlichen Aufsätzen, Dissertationen und Fachbüchern.

Visit us on the internet:

http://www.grin.com/

http://www.facebook.com/grincom

http://www.twitter.com/grin_com

Bergische Universität Wuppertal

Amerikanistik

SS 10

Selected American Plays

The two faces of the character Blanche DuBois in

A Streetcar Named Desire

BA

4. Semester

Table of contents

1.   Introduction

This paper is going to be a written report of my presentation of *A Streetcar Named Desire* given in one of the classes of the course 'Selected American Plays'.

The play has many different characters from which I chose the character Blanche DuBois since she seemed to be the most interesting one when I read the play.

In this paper I want to pay special attention to what I titled "the two faces of Blanche DuBois": she pretends to be innocent and good while she actually has a very striking past implying death, unhappy sexual relationships and alcoholic abuse, which she wants to hide from other people and which causes her to be on a desperate quest for somebody who sees her as something special and who unconditionally loves and protects her.

In my analysis of Blanche DuBois I am going to observe her outer appearance, her behavior concerning men and I am going to discuss the meaning of different themes in the play such as bathing, light or alcohol.

2.   Outer appearance

Blanche's outer appearance is remarkable for how she pretends to be. Right in the beginning of the play she is introduced as being "incongruous to this setting" (Williams 2338) since the play is set in a corner of lower class New Orleans and Blanche looks like "she were arriving at a summer tea or cocktail party in the garden district" (Williams 2338). She is dressed completely in white with "earrings of pearl", "gloves" and a "hat" (Williams 2338) and reminds the reader of a "moth" (Williams 2338). Her white clothes symbolize innocence since white is a color which stands for "innocence and purity" as David Johnson explains it in his online article about Color Psychology (Johnson). Blanche's choice of style shows that she is used to be part of a life of the higher classes of society, a life which pretends to be a party.

Patricia Hern writes in her commentary on the play that "the images associated with Blanche generally imply fragile beauty" (Hern xi). This implication was also present when the play had its premiere at theater with actress Jessica Tandy as Blanche. Tandy got the role because of her "fragile appearance" (Kolin 19), looking "the way Williams imagined Blanche should – trim, pale, graceful, sophisticated" (Kolin 18). During the play, Blanche always takes care to look good and she does not want to be looked at when she feels sweaty or dirty. At her reunion with Stella, Blanche tells her sister not to "look at [her], […] not till [she has] bathed and rested" (Williams 2340). In the scene of the poker night, Blanche tells Stella to "wait till [she powders]" before introducing Blanche to Stanley's friends, because she feels "so hot and frazzled". She does not want to "look done in" (Williams 2353). When Stella tells her, that she looks "fresh as a daisy", Blanche's answer "one that's been picked a few days" (Williams 2353) shows that she knows that she becomes older and that she thinks her beauty is fading like a picked flower fades. It underlines how Blanche "longs to be protected against the dangers of fading physical beauty and old age" (Hern xxxviii). When *A Streetcar Named Desire*" was made into a movie, actress Vivien Leigh "portrayed Blanche" fittingly "as a sophisticated lady played out – fighting wrinkles and loneliness" (Kolin 155).

Stella is aware of the fact that all this admiration and telling how beautiful she looks "is important with Blanche". She describes it as her "little weakness" when she advises Stanley to "admire [Blanche's] dress" and to "tell her she's looking wonderful" (Williams 2347).

Also Blanche other clothes represent what seems to be important for her. When Stanley pulls open her wardrobe trunk, he finds "feathers and furs", "a solid-gold dress", "white fox-pieces", "pearls", "bracelets of solid gold" and "a rhinestone tiara" (Williams 2348). These are all material things which make a woman look beautiful and rich. What it does not show is how the woman – in this case Blanche – looks from the inside and what she tries to hide. The rhinestone tiara which Blanche "wore for a costume ball" (Williams 2348) gives a hint that all these nice things are just superficial and that Blanche's whole life is a fake, just like her faked identity at the costume ball.

Her inside, which she tries to hide from all people, is the contrast of her beautiful outer appearance. Several experiences in her life ruined it, the first being the discovery of the homosexual affair of her husband with another man and his following suicide, (cf. Williams 2375) which made her start drinking alcohol in order to cover and forget bad things ("afterward we pretended that nothing had been discovered.[…] very drunk and laughing" Williams 2375). Nicholas Pagan résumés that Blanche "conceals this fact, hides it beneath her white apparel and beneath her name" (Pagan 66).

3.   In company of men

The play shows different situations wherein Blanche is in company of men. Similar to her outer appearance, she shows a behavior with whom she tries to hide the dark side of her inner self.

The first man she has a conversation with is Stanley. While Stella is in the bathroom, Stanley comes home from work and meets Blanche for the first time. "Drawing involuntary back from his stare" (Williams 2345), she seems to feel uncomfortable in his presence. She does not want him to think badly of her so she excuses herself for not "looking fresh" and that she should have "washed or […] powered [her] face" (Williams 2345) which shows that it is very important for her that men find her beautiful and admire her instead of staring at her. When one reads that Stanley "sizes women up at a glance, with sexual classifications, crude images flashing into his mind and determining the way he smiles at them" (Williams 2345), one can interpret that Blanche does not like to be looked at in that way because she does not want to be just an object of sexual desire but she wants to be truly loved by someone who is "gentle" (Williams 2386) and gallant ("I appreciate your gallantry" Williams 2357).

This wish results from her experiences with men in the past. It started with her husband Allan Grey whom she married at the age of sixteen (cf. Williams 2375) and whom she loved and "adored" so much that she almost "worshipped the ground he walked on" (Williams 2379). Their marriage was ended by him killing himself (cf. Williams 2375) after she found out about his homosexual affair and informed him about her feelings by telling him that he disgusts her (cf. Williams 2376). The shocking suicide might have triggered her behavior of avoiding telling people her true feelings whenever it is possible.

The following years, she always had trouble because of her strange relationships with men, having started with a love affair with "a seventeen-year-old boy [..] she'd gotten mixed up with" (Williams 2378) while she was a teacher at the young boy's high school. After the boy's father found out, the person responsible for the school "kicked her out […] before the spring term ended" (Williams 2378). Here, one can find one of Blanche's lies to cover what had happened by telling people that she "[resigned] temporarily from the high school because of her nerves" (Williams 2378) or by not telling at all that she does not teach any more ("I teach high school. In Laurel." Williams 2357).

In scene five, when Blanche is alone at the Kowalski's home, one notices that she is remembering that particular student when a young collector comes along. Although she does not know him at all, she acts seductively in his presence and kisses him (cf. Williams 2370). Then, probably aware of his age and what she has just done, she tells him that she has to "keep [her] hand off children" (Williams 2370) and sends him away.

"Seeking sanctuary" (Thompson 30) and "to combat her sense of loneliness, isolation, and restlessness" (Heintzelman 29), she does not find "a soul mate, but only promiscuous 'intimacies with strangers'" (Thompson 30). This relates to her affairs with many different men who stayed in a hotel called the "Flamingo" (Williams 2377), a "second-class hotel which has the advantage of not interfering in the private social life of the personalities", so says Stanley (Williams 2377). According to what he got to know and tells Stella, Blanche was some kind of prostitute, a nymphomaniac woman who therefore became a "town character" and was "practically told by the mayor to get out of town" (Williams 2377). These parts of the play underline in the tradition of the stories of the Wild West the "idea of women either as child-bearers and home-makers or as whores" whereby Blanche is in contrast to Stella neither of the first two things, thus she "might [...] be expected to be one of the other kind" (Hern xix).

Blanche tries to hide this part of her life and pretends to be an innocent woman who does not have much experience with men. Philip C. Kolin describes her as "Madonna and Venus" in one person, as "a hallowed representative of the Old South, a secular saint" on the one hand and as "a nymphomaniac, a liar, an infectious source of destructive feminine desire" (Kolin 3) on the other hand. Judith J. Thompson compares her to "the entire biblical epic of human degeneration, from Eve-like innocence to the Whore of Babylon" (Thompson 31).

The point of pretending not to have much experience with men leads to another important man in Blanche's life: Mitch, Stanley's co-worker and friend. When Blanche and Mitch meet for the first time during the poker night, Mitch is "delighted" (Williams 2357) by her and Blanche is also a little bit impressed by him because he seems "superior to the others" and has "a sort of sensitive look" (Williams 2354). The scene is a first shy flirt between the two of them. Blanche presents herself from her best side e.g. by translating her French name into "white woods" (Williams 2356). Hereby she wants to underline her innocence and wants "to make her world white, pure, innocent, virginal" (Pagan 65). Blanche always takes care of holding up the positive picture Mitch has got about her ("I like you exactly the way you are [...] – I have never known anyone like you" Williams 2371) because she

6

feels that he could be the right man to spend her life with. According to Thompson, her effort for a relationship with Mitch is "a diminished version" of her "romantic attempt to achieve an idyllic union with Allan Grey" (Thompson 33). Blanche thinks that Mitch would be a good husband because they "have both been anxious and solemn" and they both need somebody to hold on to. Blanche wants "to create […] *joie de vivre*" for the future; she "[needs] somebody […] – a cleft in the rock of the world that [she can] hide in" (Williams 2386). Besides love she longs for protection – which is according to a quote of film director Kazan in Patricia Hern's commentary "her chief motivation" (Hern xxxvii) - and Blanche thinks that Mitch is somebody who can offer both of these two things. So Blanche pretends to be a woman Mitch would like to marry. She pays him compliments ("you're a natural gentleman, one of the very few left in the world" Williams 2373) and pretends to have "old-fashioned ideals" (Williams 2373) which means that in Mitch's presence she refuses to do anything that goes beyond a kiss. This makes her seem pure and clean like a virgin. When Mitch finds out the truth about her, he does not want to marry her anymore because of all the "lies" (Williams 2387) and because she is "not clean enough to bring in the house with [his] mother" (Williams 2388).

At the climax of the play, right before Stanley rapes Blanche, she tries to tell lies again by saying that the relationship of her and Mitch came to an end not because of Mitch refusing her but because of her breaking up with him due to "[their] attitudes and [their] backgrounds" which are "incompatible" (Williams 2390). In front of Stanley, she cannot hold up the picture she wants everybody to see of her because he found out that everything she said were "lies and conceit and tricks" (Williams 2391).

After the rape, Blanche's personality is totally destroyed and she is lost in her imagination ("I can smell the sea air. The rest of my time I'm going to spend on the sea." Williams, 2395) and in her wish to be completely pure and clean ("I'll be buried […] in a clean white sack" Williams 2395). She tries to "achieve an ideal in a 'broken world'" (Thompson 30). Her wish for a "clean, bright funeral" is "like a return to youthful romance" (Hern xxxix). Always remembering her first love ("dropped […] into an ocean as blue as […] my first lover's eyes" Williams, 2395), she hopes for "eternal happiness in heaven" (Hern xxxix).

The last man Blanche meets in the play is the Doctor who comes to bring her to an asylum. He finally seems to be the man Blanche waited for. Since she has "always depended on the kindness of strangers" (Williams 2397), she trusts the Doctor with his "gentle" voice (Williams 2397) and understanding smile. He is her perfect gentleman who "supports her with his arm and leads her through the portieres" (Williams 2397), guiding her out on the street to bring her to the asylum.

4.   Important Symbols

4.1   Bathing

Reading *A Streetcar Named Desire*, one gets the impression that Blanche is constantly bathing and one wonders why she needs to "[soak] herself in a hot tube" while it is "temperature 100 on the nose" (Williams 2376) as Stanley says.

According to Blanche, "a hot bath [...] always [gives her] a brand new outlook on life" (Williams 2380) and it helps "to quiet her nerves" (Williams 2346) as Stella notes.

The actual reason for her many bathes is that she desires to cleanse her moral self which got dirty by her immoral lifestyle with its many affairs. While she is bathing, she sings lines from different songs which always talk about unrequited love ("But it wouldn't be make-believe If you believed in me!" "Without your love, It's a honky-tonk parade!" Williams 2377) and which therefore reflect her desire for someone who loves her as much as she loves him. When Blanche takes a bath, she can imagine that everything in her life goes well, she can forget reality for a moment and imagine to be an innocent child again ("little breathless cries and peals of laughter are heard as if a child were frolicking in the tub" Williams 2378).

According to what Patricia Hern says is Blanche neither able to "free herself from the contradictions of her own nature nor [to] shake off the burden of guilt she has carried ever since her husband's death" (Hern xxxix) and so she is never done with the cleaning process of bathing.

4.2   Light

Blanche tries to avoid bright light throughout the play. For Blanche, her husband Allan Grey was the brightest light in her life, "a blinding light on something that had always been half in the shadow" (Williams 2375) and when he decided to commit suicide, this light "was turned off" (Williams 2376). Since then, Blanche cannot stand bright light (cf. Williams 2357). She always makes sure not to be seen in it. Therefore she dims the light bulb in Stanley and Stella's bedroom by having Mitch put a paper lantern over it (Williams

2357) and she never goes on a date "after six" or to "some place that's not lighted much" (Williams 2385). According to Pagan, she is "a creature of the night" and she hides "something dark" (Pagan 66). Blanche's aversion to light goes so far that authors of other books name a certain dimmed light after her ("not the harsh light outside the pub at home, but a Blanche du Bois light" Verney 7). Another reason for her dislike is her fear that someone, in particular Mitch, sees her fading beauty and therefore does not like her. Additionally, the bright light stands for a source which uncovers what was in the shadow, meaning these things of Blanche's past which she wants to hide. Pagan explains that "a naked light bulb might reveal truths about her sexual history like her predilection for boys and the fact that she has enjoyed so much sexual freedom" (Pagan 70). So she uses dimmed light to pretend to be innocent and younger and fresher than she actually is.

4.3   Alcohol

Alcohol in Blanche's life is – similar to bathing – a source for trying to forget what has happened. It starts right in the beginning of the play, when Blanche arrives at the Kowalski's home and Stanley and Stella are not there, yet. Blanche is shocked because her sister Stella is living in a totally different, worse area than she imagined and to calm herself down she "pours a half tumbler of whiskey and tosses it down" (Williams 2339).

In scene six, one can find the reason why Blanche started to misuse alcohol. After she found out about the affair of her husband "in the worst of all possible ways" (Williams 2375), her husband, his homosexual friend and Blanche "drove out to Moon Lake Casino, very drunk and laughing all the way" and they "pretended that nothing had been discovered" (Williams 2375). Blanche denies reality; she wants "magic" (Williams 2386) and uses alcohol to flee from reality.

Since Blanche's troubled past is present throughout the play, she is not able to stop drinking ("drinking […] went on" Williams 2388) because she needs to calm down her nerves with it ("my […] nerves broke" "this buzzes right through me and feels so *good*" (Williams 2341). After the rape, the alcohol is the only thing which can hold her up – she does not want to eat something to strengthen herself but she only wants "a drink" (Williams 2393).

Although she drinks secretly sometimes, for example in the first scene when she "carefully replaces the bottle and washes out the humbler at the sink" (Williams 2339), and although

9

she tells her sister that she "hasn't turned into a drunkard" (Williams 2340), the symptoms are clear so that Stella notices Blanche's problems and advises her not to "take another drink" (Williams 2368).

Blanche is aware of her problem and she knows that alcoholic abuse is not liked by people. Therefore she tries to make other people believe that she does not drink too much alcohol but that she "rarely touched it" (Williams 2345) and that "two is the limit" (Williams 2356).

5.   Conclusion

As one could see, Blanche is a woman full of secrets and denials who pretends to be a better person than she actually is. She experienced a lot of tragedy in her life and so she builds up her own reality. For her, life is a party with dancing, alcohol and flirting with men. She wants people to love and protect her and is constantly searching for someone who shows her this love by paying her compliments or admiring her. She uses different sources to forget reality and everything she says is expressed to make people see only her good side. Her effort of holding up a false image of herself as a better person is destroyed in the end and she leaves the scene as a broken woman who is apart from the real world in her mind.

References

Primary Literature

Williams, Tennessee., et al., eds. *The Norton Anthology of American Literature*. Ed. Nina Baym, et al. 7th shorter ed. New York: Norton & Company, 2008. 2337-2398

Secondary Literature

Heintzelman, Greta and Alycia Smith Howard: *Critical Companion to Tennessee Williams: A Literary Reference to His Life and Work*. New York: Facts On File, Inc., 2005.

Hern, Patricia: "Commentary and Notes". *Tennessee Williams: A Streetcar Named Desire*. Reading: Cox & Wyman Ltd., 1984. xiv-xlviii)

Johnson, David: "Color Psychology." Infoplease. © 2000–2007 Pearson Education, publishing as Infoplease.15 Dec. 2010 <http://www.infoplease.com/spot/colors1.html#ixzz18DRz4xey>.

Kolin, Philip C. *Williams: A Streetcar Named Desire*. Cambridge: Cambridge University Press, 2000.

Pagan, Nicholas: *Rethinking Literary Biography: A Postmodern Approach to Tennessee Williams*. Cranbury: Associated University Presses, Inc., 1993.

Thompson, Judith J. *Tennessee Williams's Plays: Memory, Myth, Symbol*. New York: Peter Lang Publishing, Inc., 2002

Verney, Jay: *Percussion*. St. Lucia: University of Queensland Press, 2004.